Story by Thornton Cline
Illustrations by Susan Oliver

ISBN: 978-1-57424-361-1
SAN 683-8022

Cover by James Creative Group
All Illustrations by Susan Oliver

P.O. Box 17878 - Anaheim Hills, CA 92817

www.centerstream-usa.com

"The Amazing Incredible Shrinking Saxophone" is a fun and engaging story inspiring students to practice. For a young student, this book will be very memorable because of the creative writing, musical samples and illustrations. I love that Thornton has the ability to capture the imagination through the eyes of a child. Some of my students could have used a shrinking saxophone!"

– Pattie Cossentino, Professional Saxophone player

"A good lesson for young musicians and some fun tunes to play, all in one book."

– Jim Geiger, Band Director, Portland Middle School

The
Amazing
Incredible
Shrinking
Saxophone

Dylan was a stubborn boy. He liked to build things.

When he made up his mind about how something was supposed to be—that's how it was—end of discussion.

Dylan loved the sound of the alto saxophone when it played jazz music.

"Jazz is my favorite," he told his friends.

"I want to play the alto saxophone," he told his mom and dad.

Dylan's parents agreed to let him play alto saxophone if he would practice.

"We've signed you up for band at school," his mom said.

"And we've found a good private saxophone teacher for you," his dad said.

"Awesome."

Dylan met his new band teacher, Mr. Adams who taught the students how to play their instruments.

"This is your new book of songs," Mr. Adams said.

"One, two, three, four,
play B flat whole note,
B flat whole note,
B flat whole note,"
Mr. Adams said.

Dylan was bored with playing whole notes. He made up his own song while the others were playing.

Mr. Adams stopped the class.

"What are you doing? You're supposed to be playing songs from the book."

"That's baby stuff. I want to play jazz."

Mr. Adams lost his patience with Dylan.

"Dylan, I'll see you after class."

After class, Mr. Adams talked to Dylan about his behavior.

"Dylan, you must never, ever play or talk while I'm teaching."

"I'm bored because they don't sound like songs," Dylan replied.

"You have to start with easy songs if you want to be good on the saxophone. That's how you learn," Mr. Adams said.

Dylan didn't listen to Mr. Adams. He was determined to learn jazz all by himself.

A week later, Dylan had his lesson with Ms. Kelly.

"Turn to page six and play this song," she said.

Dylan played his saxophone.

"One, two, three, four, half note B flat, half note B flat, half note B flat," Ms. Kelly said.

Before she could finish, Dylan put his saxophone in his lap.

"Why did you stop?" Asked Ms. Kelly.

"I don't want to play this easy stuff," Dylan said.

"What do you want to play?"

"I want to play jazz."

"You've got to play this before you can play the hard songs."

"But why?"

"The easy songs prepare you for the harder ones. You'll be able to play jazz later."

Dylan didn't listen to Ms. Kelly. He wanted to play jazz now.

Ms. Kelly told him he would need to play the songs she asked him to if he was going to study with her.

But Dylan didn't listen.

Dylan continued his stubborn and rude behavior for weeks. Mr. Adams and Ms. Kelly were ready to ask him to quit.

After school, as Dylan was walking home, an old man played his saxophone on the corner. Dylan stopped and listened. The man was very good. He played difficult jazz songs. Dylan's eyes grew wide.

“I want to play like that!”

The man laughed.

“My dear boy, do you know how long it took me to play like that?”

“How long?”

“It took a long time—many years.”

“You’re kidding.”

“I kid you not,” he said.

“I started like you. I wanted to play jazz the moment I got my sax. But I had to wait patiently. I had to practice the easy songs my teachers gave me and work my way up to being a pro jazz player.

"My teachers won't let me play jazz."

"If you keep up your attitude of not cooperating with your teachers and not playing the songs they ask you to play, your saxophone will shrink to such a small size that you won't be able to play it anymore," he warned.

"How do you know so much about me?"

"I know a lot about you Dylan," he said.

"Are you a ghost or an angel?"

"Something like that," he said.

Weeks passed and Dylan still refused to play the easy songs Mr. Adams and Ms. Kelly assigned.

One day he noticed his saxophone was getting smaller than before.

“Your saxophone is shrinking,” his friend said in class.

“No way, saxophones don’t shrink,” Dylan said.

But Dylan's saxophone was shrinking to such a tiny size that Dylan couldn't play. He was too embarrassed to bring it to class or to his lessons. He told his teachers he lost his saxophone.

Dylan knew he had to do something if he was going to ever play again.

Could the old man on the street corner have been right—my saxophone could be shrinking? He thought.

He tried to play his saxophone again but it was difficult since it was so tiny.

Dylan started playing the easy songs his teachers had taught him. After lots of practice, his saxophone started to grow until it was big enough to take to class and lessons.

“If you keep playing like that you will be playing jazz one day,” Mr. Adams said.

Dylan continued to follow his teachers’ direction until he got so good that his teachers felt he was ready to play some jazz songs. His dream was coming true, and he was even having fun.

Dylan told his mom and dad, "I went back to that same street corner to find the old man saxophone player, but he wasn't there.

I wanted to tell him he was right, you've got to learn how to play the easy songs before you can play the hard ones. I'm having fun playing the songs Mr. Adams and Ms. Kelly taught me."

"And now I'm playing jazz! Thanks Mom, Dad and my teachers. Maybe some day I'll even have a band of my own!"

THE END.

Song Titles

(PLEASE note that all piano chords in songs are written a major sixth down from the alto saxophone melodies.)

My Saxophone

Thornton Cline

Before You Play The Hard Ones

Thornton Cline

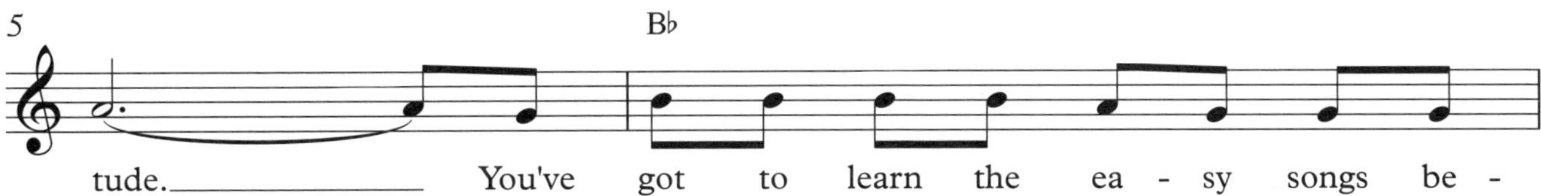

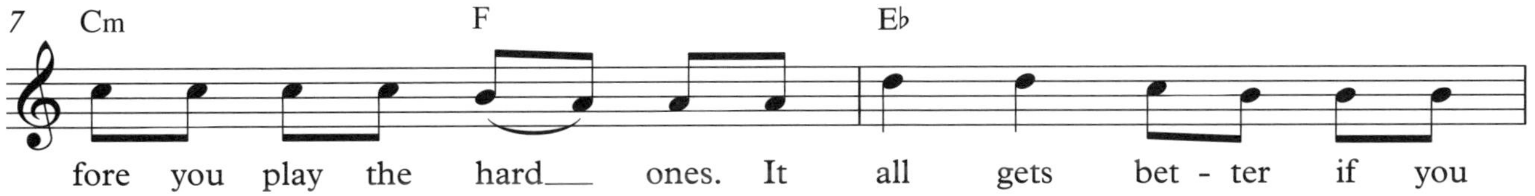

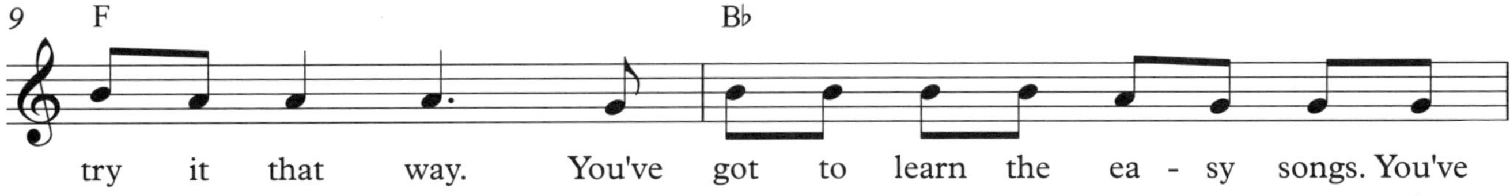

I Want To Play Like That

Your Saxophone Will Shrink

Thornton Cline

My Saxophone Is Shrinking

Do Something

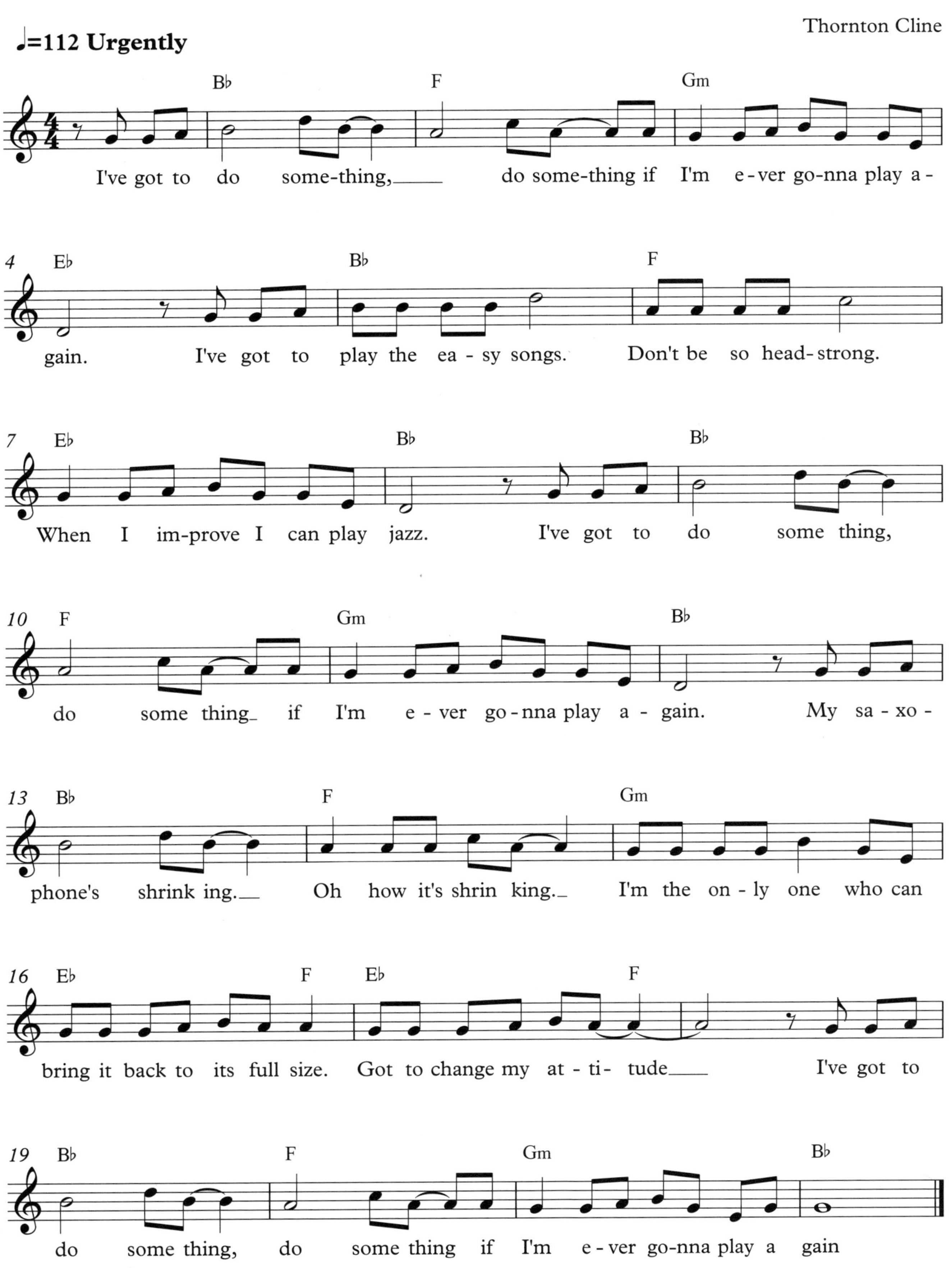

I Want To Play Jazz

If You Keep Playing Like That

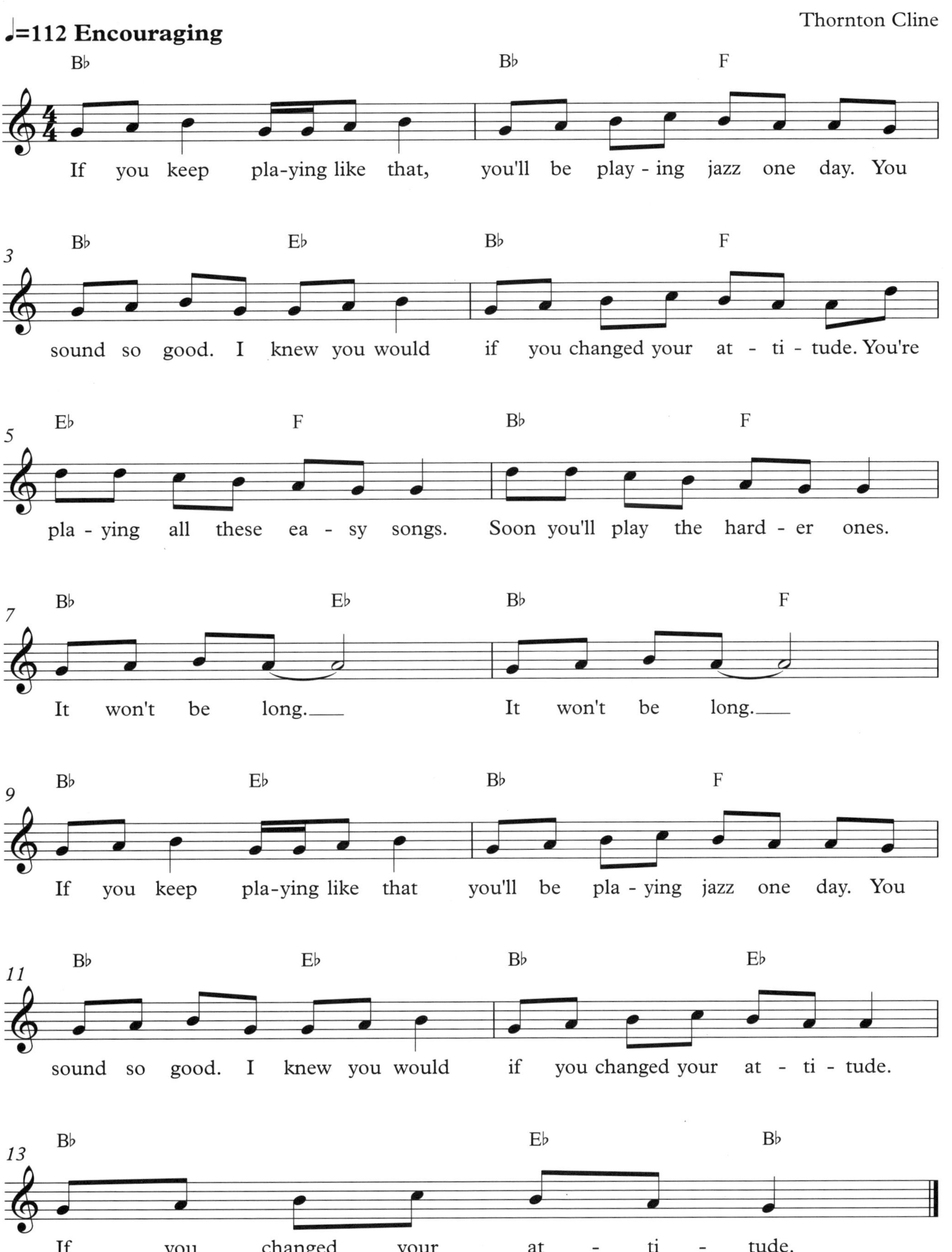

My Teachers Let Me Play Some Jazz Songs

Thornton Cline

I Can Play Jazz

Thornton Cline

♩=102 Confidently

E♭ B♭

I can play jazz.___ I can play jazz.___ It

3 F B♭

took lots of pa - tience and time.

5 E♭ B♭

Play - ing all those ea - sy songs, made my pla - ying grow___ strong.

7 E♭ F

Now I own the sa - xo - phone, it's mine.

9 E♭ B♭

I can play jazz.___ I can play jazz.___ It

11 F B♭

took lots of pa - tience and time.

13 E♭ B♭

I can play jazz.___ I can play jazz.___ It

15 F B♭

took lots of pa - tience and time.________ It

17 F B♭

took lots of pa - tience and time.

Biographies

Thornton Cline is author of eighteen books: *Band of Angels, Practice Personalities: What's Your Type? Practice Personalities for Adults, The Contrary, The Amazing Incredible Shrinking Violin, The Amazing Incredible Shrinking Piano, The Amazing Incredible Shrinking Guitar, The Amazing Musical Magical Plants, A Travesty of Justice, Not My Time to Go, The Amazing Incredible Shrinking Ukulele, The Amazing Incredible Shrinking Trumpet, Perfectly Precious Poolichious, Poohlicious: Look at Me!, Because I Can, El Increible sorprendente violin que se encogia, The Amazing Incredible Shrinking Drums* and Cline's eighteenth children's book, *The Amazing Incredible Shrinking Saxophone.* Thornton Cline has been honored with "Songwriter of the Year" twice in a row by the Tennessee Songwriter's Association for his hit song, "Love is the Reason," recorded by Engelbert Humperdinck and Gloria Gaynor. Cline has received Dove and Grammy Award nominations for his songs. Most recently, Cline has been honored with the Maxy Award for "Children's Book of the Year 2017". Thornton Cline is an in-demand author, teacher, speaker, clinician, performer and songwriter. He lives in Hendersonville, Tennessee with his wife, Audrey.

Susan Oliver is an award-winning songwriter and visual artist as well as illustrator. She is originally from Orono, Maine and attended the University of Maine as well as Portland School of Art. Known for her wide variety of styles, Susan has exhibited her artwork and also worked as a graphic designer. Her painting, "Moonlight Seals" gained national attention in efforts to raise funds for Marine Animal Lifeline, an organization dedicated to seal rescue and rehabilitation. Susan now resides outside of Nashville, Tennessee where she continues to write music and design art work for album covers for various musical artists, as well as illustrates children's books. *The Amazing Incredible Shrinking Saxophone* is Oliver's ninth children's book published as an illustrator.

Credits

Audrey

Mollie Cline

Alex Cline

God

Susan Oliver, illustrations

Ron Middlebrook

Sumner Academy

Cumberland Arts Academy

Marcelo Cataldo, transcriber

Crystal Bowman, editing

Mary Elizabeth Jackson, editing

Hendersonville Christian Academy

Gallatin Creative Arts Center

Clinetel Music

Lawrence Boothby, photography

Cumberland University

Roberta Cline

Another Amazing Book!

“The rousing climax will delight and entertain all”
– Nancy and Randall Faber

“Sweet story, well written”!
– Marlene Tachoir

THE AMAZING MAGICAL MUSICAL PLANTS

Story by Thornton Cline & Crystal Bowman, Illustrations by Susan Oliver

Mr. Jones is having trouble motivating his fifth grade band students to practice. When he discovers a packet of magical musical plant seeds in an old trombone case, he gets an idea. Mr. Jones plants the seeds in pots of soil and gives one to each of his students to take home. He tells the students how to care for the seeds and to play their instruments every day to make the plants grow. Some of his students laugh at his crazy idea, but some of his students take him seriously. The whimsical illustrations by acclaimed illustrator Susan Oliver add to the charm of this delightful story. The book includes a CD of ten easy original songs with recorded examples of each instrument. (Recommended for ages 4-8)

00155787 Book/CD Pack...$19.99

P.O. Box 17878 - Anaheim Hills, CA 92817

(714) 779-9390   www.centerstream-usa.com

More Great Books from Thornton Cline...

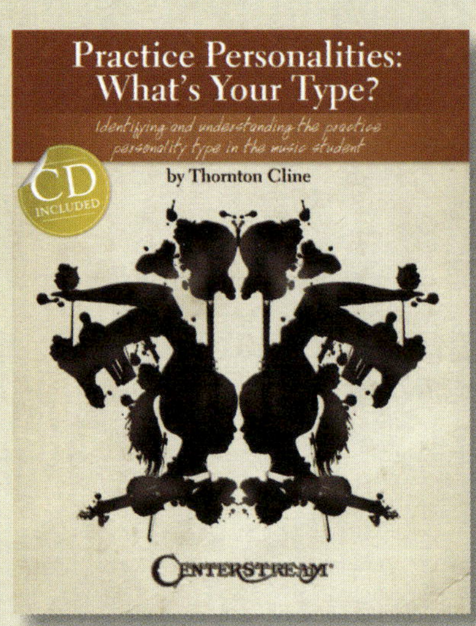

PRACTICE PERSONALITIES: WHAT'S YOUR TYPE?

Identifying and Understanding the Practice Personality Type in the Music Student

by Thornton Cline

Teaching is one of the greatest responsibilities in society. It's an art form that requires craft, patience, creativity, and intelligence. Practice Personalities: What's Your Type? will help teachers, parents and students realize the challenges of practicing, understand the benefits of correct practicing, identify and understand nine practice personality types, and employ useful strategies to effectively motivate and inspire each type of student. The accompanying CD demonstrates effective practice strategies for selected piano, violin and guitar excerpts from the book.

00101974 Book/CD Pack $24.99

Companion DVD Available

00121577 DVD $19.99

PRACTICE PERSONALITIES FOR ADULTS

Identifying and Understanding the Practice Personality Type in the Adult Music Student

by Thornton Cline

Did you know that your personality can affect the way you learn and perform on a musical instrument? This book identifies nine practice personalities in music students. Adults will learn how to practice more effectively and efficiently according to their personalities. A Practice Personalities test is included along with an accompanying CD.

00131613 Book/CD Pack $24.99

P.O. Box 17878 - Anaheim Hills, CA 92817

(714) 779-9390 www.centerstream-usa.com